Fragrance Of The Undaunted Soul

A Garden of Creative Thoughts and
Inspirational Emotions

Deimaphi Dashisha Wanswett

Dedication

I dedicate this book of poems to my husband, Richard Jyrwa, who is a wonderful father to our daughter, whose faithfulness has established my desire to write to my heart's content.

 To my daughter, Qezia Huldah Wanswett, 'Qezia' meaning 'Resilience', the pure love in her eyes has given me the ability to withstand challenges every day.

 To my mother, Holda Wanswett, whose Self-sacrificing love has created in me an eagerness to be a good person despite my flaws.

 To my eldest sister, a role model for strength, selflessness and mental fortitude. Her ability to navigate life's challenges with grace is indeed inspirational.

 To my elder brother, who has always been kind, big-hearted and trustworthy. A man of integrity and emotional intelligence, a father figure, a respectful gentleman whose faith in God is also an inspiration.

 And especially to My Lord and Saviour Jesus Christ, the source of love and light in my life. My maker, whose presence is worthy of all my sincere praise. I am thankful to Him for giving me this gift and the ability to be creative.

 My capabilities begins with Him, so, when I am face to face with adversity, I am content in His compassion.

Preface

Welcome to the Fragrance of the Undaunted Soul

This is a garden where the Fragrance of the Undaunted Soul will succumb your fears in a subtle manner.

Fragrances can trigger a fond distant memory, they can keep a wonderful moment alive, with the ability to soothe the subconscious mind.
A familiar scent can cause a memory to reappear; the fragrance of my undaunted soul comes in the form of my poetry, which I hope, will have a calming effect on you. I hope my poetry will be remembered as an aromatherapeutic product, where one day we'll wake up to find my words have lingered on, absorbed in our senses and taken us back in time.

A fragrance can immortalize a special moment, seeping into the fragments of our clothes or fabrics and sometimes the pages of a book. Scents can also trigger flashbacks which can refuel and restore soul-ties with particular people. It can create a bridge connecting from those past unspoken memories of preferred places to the blessed paths of present reality. They can create a firm attachment to a fellow human being or the person you fell in love with. Fragrances are the invisible fine embroidery of sweet smelling flowers and naturally delicious fruits of a human life.

A scent has the ability to speak to our minds with rapturous joy and ignite a fire of strong emotions that have been held back for far too long.

Fragrance of the Undaunted Soul is about the untamed personality, the innocence and the forgotten beauty of a human being that has not been indoctrinated by the rules of superficial lifestyle and the expectations of modern society. This book is about a heart that is not discouraged by bleak experiences.

An escape from authoritarian ideas that might have been indirectly dictating the way we think.

In Fragrance of the Undaunted Soul, each individual is being encouraged to extract their abilities and to showcase their creative expressions which might have been buried and forgotten; these poems remind the readers to bring out the beauty of their original self, a Self that craves to discover his/her true potentialities and to live a happy life, unafraid of what other people might say.

The fragrance that you hold could be one of a kind, unique or with properties limited to only a few individuals. These kinds of fragrances need to be shared with the world in order to bring hope and joy to someone, somewhere. This book is a solace which will bring joy to other creative thinkers, to talk of and talk about their hidden fragrances.

While reading these poems, I hope the Fragrance of my Undaunted Soul will carry you to a safe place, away from your struggles and self doubts, after all we are all God's work of art. I hope it will give you an insight on how to unveil the gift of your imagination, some verse will lead your heart closer to God and some will help you realise how important it is to embrace yourself, for being different. Some lines are meant to let you think delicately about love, some to take you on nature-walks and discover spiritual growth, while some verses are home-made remedies which might help you heal from your past traumatic experiences.

- Deimaphi Dashisha Wanswett

Acknowledgements

 To my husband, Richard, who keeps on reminding me
from time to time to embrace my gift, to be different and
exceptional.
Having him as my life partner is a blessing because he
understands my overwhelming emotions. His
encouragement and prayers have always been a guiding
light towards my purpose.

 To my mother who has nurtured and loved me
unconditionally and in maintaining a thankful heart no
matter the circumstances.

 Most importantly, To my heavenly Father, my Lord and
Saviour Jesus Christ whose never-ending grace and
unconditional love has strengthened my wearied human
heart and for giving me the gift to write and express my
emotions through creative writing and poetry.

 As a poet, I take pleasure in acknowledging the gracious
publisher in opening this runway for passionate writers
to share our gift with the world.

1. The Yarn of an Introvert's Divergent Nature

The Yellow-Pond Lily travels and struggles,
It struggles through a solitary path,
But it would never let the calling
of her imagination go unanswered.

Her nature-walks offers a deep cleanse,
Away from all the vulnerability and chaos.
An eye-catching stream caught
her beautiful brown eyes,
She walks on towards her favourite spot,
A heart-catching pond,
Not merely an eye-catching one.
She sat down, surrendering to the calm.

Dipped her feet under the cool water,
Where the Yellow-Pond Lily tells her a story,
The tadpoles at the pond tries to nibble at her toes,
But they can only lightly touch the skin of a wearied
soul.

Oh! to have an introvert's divergent quality,
Always finding renewed strength in all creation,
Acknowledging the beautifully intricate shape of the

pebbles and the stones.

In the perseverance of Wildflowers,
Who need no tending from human hands,
They are a calm reminder,
Of the great Creator,
Taking good care of all their requirements;
They bloom to remind humans,
Of our ineffective strategies,
Towards our meaningless worries,
They cover the earth so beautifully,
Cleansing away all of our compulsive attributes.

When evening comes,
She walks back home,
In the accompaniment of the bees.
The Vanilla fragrance oil she wears,
Unpretentiously yet formally invites the bees,
While enhancing the beauty of her Collarbone.

The house Sparrows began their evening meeting,
Deciding whose turn it was to watch and spy,
With peering eyes, they meet the skies.

From underneath the cosy roof of her home,
The house Sparrows can hear the tea kettle
Whistling and beaming with life;

The smell of Hibiscus tea filled her homely kitchen,
A kitchen with lemon-honey coloured wall cabinets.
Vases filled with Sweet Alyssum, Dianthus and
Delphiniums usher the bees to the dining table.

The colours of the sunset sky,
Pumping more blood into her heart,
Sending essential air into her lungs.
The fragrance of the Yellow-Pond lily,
Embraced her quirky personality,
From May to October wholeheartedly.

A conversation with the Yellow-Pond Lily,
Now forever embedded in her journal
Of life-altering observations and intimate reflections.

2. Fragrance Of The Undaunted Soul

The simple things in life are imperishable riches,
Riches residing in the fibres and muscles of a creative
mind.
The little things revealed in nature,
The extraordinary answers in ordinary wonders;
Inspiration does not stand on the edges of an artist's
mind.
In truth it lies at the core and direct her choices.

A gifted soul can hear a faith-call from a distance.
The desirable confrontation with our emotions
Will have to happen before we leave this world.
For now we know,
A striving soul can transcend the dark skies.

Exceptional minds have a special kind of artistry.
A Writer's pure conception,
A Painter's message behind his masterpiece;
A Quilter's choice fabric in making a quilt.

In the hands of a gardener and a baker,
Lies a treasure yet to be discovered.
Created with an eagerness to taste grace,

One of a kind design in each fingerprint,
Touched the batter while baking,
Touched the earth while gardening,
Mixed with invisible extraordinary energy,
Connected beyond our human case of the ordinary.

In a land called, the 'Abode of clouds',
A declaration of determination,
Came to be,
A mighty voice in her conscience,
Speaks softly but firmly,
To subdue and hush,
The perpetrators of the human mind,
In order to enrich, to affectionately enhance,
The fragrance of the undaunted soul.
In order to reach a secret compartment,
Hidden away in the heart of a young poet,
A series of mindful experiences must be preserved.

All the intimidating noises,
And all the threatening nervousness,
Must be nipped in the bud,
Like pinching off a pest-infected flower bud,
To prevent a negative thought from escalating.
To magnify a beautiful soul,
To secure a roaring desire,

To conceive what the soul seeks,
To set the fragrance of the undaunted soul free.

6

3. Love From Inside the Alabaster Jar

They say, 'True love is rare'
Most people find it only once.
This is about a friend,
Who kindly asked me,
To tell his tragic story.

True love calls for sacrifice,
Fret not,
For fearless hearts are called to be tested.

When the strings of a musical instrument
comes alive,
Reveries started pouring from his dry bones.
He goes to a place in time,
A place where he first held her hand.

He wanted to recite a fading reluctant memory,
Recapturing the image of his true love,
His true love, one of a kind,
Walking nervously, blushing,
Softly illustrating a blossoming romance.

His subconscious mind longing for her presence,

But she is far away now,
His handkerchief painted in his delicate tears,
He listened to the wind,
With solemnly reserved ears.

He was caught breathless,
Whilst those rarest feelings remained,
They remain in an inflammable heart.
For whenever he remembered her eyes,
All rational reasoning left him.

While walking in the midst of the warm breeze,
He stopped to stand next to the Papaya plant,
Whose stem is not made as woody as a tree.
While looking at the Papaya hollow trunk,
He felt the hollow deepening in his own heart.
The first star in the sky,
Touched by the triumphant sunset,
Suddenly strikes that grievous wound.

Recapturing the past,
Refusing to move on,
The feelings came back,
But they came back without her.
For years and years he remained,
Dwelling in his own pain.

One day he woke up,
To see his scars fade away.
That pain, a healthy soil, that changed him.
Because of this predicament,
A higher calling appeared before his eyes,
Here, he starts making,
A new path, that leads to his spiritual well-being;
A heart that has never been in love,
Cannot conquer the lost and the broken.

Hearts are meant to go into the wilderness,
Hearts are meant to be broken -
To be caught with a realisation
That it was wrong when the world says,
"Follow your worldly heart,"
"Follow your worldly intuition."

To follow the over-influenced heart inevitably means to
follow the materialistic flesh,
The human heart is corrupted, deceitful and proud,
Full of regretful courses and trapped passages,
So the heart needs to break completely.

Breaking all the veins and the skin,
Breaking and opening,
Unsealing the fragrance suffocated within.
A heart broken enough,

Allowing the graceful perfume,
To seep out through the cracks and the bruises.

So, don't look for love through an uncertain door,
Look for True Love in a Saviour, there, you'll find,
Though your past is painful,
His plans, when finally unveiled,
You'll see, all that pain was meant to mould you.

Just like an Alabaster jar,
With its distinctive quality,
It holds a perfume that tells,
One of the most cherished love stories.

Of an ointment of precious Spikenard in her hands,
Of how she broke the jar to anoint His feet,
And wipe them so gently with her hair.

So, when they say, "True love is rare",
They have not yet known the rugged cross,
The love it holds,
For those abandoned, mortified and humiliated.
For those neglected, bare and unaware.

If I tell you, "Look at the cross, look at the saviour",
Would you care?

Would you learn to know?

He can give you 'True love' if only you dare.

11

4. Incomprehensible Miracle

No amount of emotional breakdown can hold you back,
Real beauty lies in the fact that we are all broken,
Meticulously in the pursuit of finding out,
If there is someone who can mend our brokenness.

To find self-worth,
The boundaries of comfort zones must be crossed.
Thrust your traumatic baggages at His feet,
There you'll see,
Your old destructive self no longer reigns.

You'll be an unexplained incomprehensible miracle,
They will see how His divine power has transformed you greatly;
No longer loveless,
Now a new creation,
A new creation moulded by the hands of an expert Crafter,
The master sculptor himself.

The most beautiful Swans,
Emerged from the trenches,
Or so I have read.
Yet, personally, I have found,

Being real to oneself is a must,
The real self, within the crust,
The soft, porous, spongy crumb, you can trust.
And now, all your rough edges,
Are actually the blueprint,
To your most beautiful self;
Those rough edges makes you a trustworthy soul.
Keep your distance from social obligated norms,
Away from edge banding heat-activated adhesive forms,
Getting better at being socially awkward,
Rather than being drown in unjust reward.

Those rough edges so uniquely designed,
Until one day they will refine and define,
The most beautiful characteristics found in you.
Now your Character is giving out a delicious smell,
Your rough edges enhanced your degree in maturity,
For without those edges,
Your beauty would be pointless.
Those rough edges so uniquely designed,
They turned out to be,
The most beautiful characteristics found in you.
Consumed by the refiner's fire,
The revival of the human soul.

5. Resuscitation of the Pressed-flower Petals

A dried oddly-shaped yellow leaf and some petals fell
from the book in her hand,
A leaf she had forgotten about,
A leaf belonging to a distant memory,
A leaf detached from a faded love story.

Her eyes caught the worn out petals,
Worn out!
But still powerful enough to emit the truth,
To make its holder go back to the past.
Worn out!
But still calmly expressing warmth.
Their courageous ability survived,
With a touch of sincerity.

Pressed in between the pages,
The only flower that holds the key,
The key to a familiar place,
Which holds the rarest love stories.
The worn out pressed flower felt,
The over-anxious sweat in her fingers,
The worn out flower still remembers.

The flower petals resuscitated a painful memory,
Of distant songs that flowed, flowed freely,
Through the wounds in her heart.
But here stands an important rhetorical question,
Must man interfere with divine intervention?

You see, the leaf and the petals did not know,
They did not think that,
Even though,
Their hearts were created to console,
They were not made to console each other.

In the blink of an eye,
A breakthrough starts to linger,
In her hurtful condition,
She hears the voice of her Saviour,
In order to resist defeat,
She must resist her past desire.

A dried-up leaf that keeps
The chaos in her heart alive,
Finally succumbed by God's grace.
Surrendered to the only one,
Who knows all, who is all powerful,
In the hands of the one
Who can transform her heavy-laden broken soul.

The flower petals pressed in between the pages,
Can dictate the weather in her heart no more.

16

6. Garden of Reveries - An Exploration inside the Mind and Imagination of a Young Lady

Modesty and Veridicality,
The reality of a woman of quality.
An undeniably unforgettable reverie
flows in her veins,
Through an ageless dream.
Absorbing the soul-wrenching memories,
Of delicate years burning in the breeze.

A woman of quality has the ability
To uncover and recreate real events,
A rescue mission to bring back the power of the
imagination,
Caged in a world of harsh facts and concrete evidences.

Watching the wind chimes curiously move,
They moved, with empathy towards the wind.
She changed her glance,
Doting on the Musk Rose blossoming in the daylight,
Weaving a garland of delight around the walls of her

home.

The soft rays of the afternoon sun surging in through the
window panes,
To touch the beauty of her face,
Compelling her to close her eyes,
Capturing these moments into an unknowingly special
memory,
The purest moment that unknowingly furbished her
eyelids.

This young maiden longed for the meadows,
To sit on the grass,
To feel the earth restored her through and through,
Witnessing bees harmonising with the flowers.

The balance of life hangs upon embellishments
Of small moments -
Of newly painted sunsets
And toe-tripping blue skies,
Of homegrown Grapefruits
And securely hand-picked Oranges,
Of consuming them with freshly plucked Mustard leaves;

If continuous construction of reveries is considered a
skill, then,
I am allowed to say,

She is equipped with the enthralling weapon of
imagination.

Her imagination glows only at specialised times,
Like fireflies at dusk and lighted lanterns rising.
It shines,
On a hot summer's night,
While she's watching the stars.
Reclining and leaning and lying down,
On the roof of her house,
The stars sailed over the skies,
Reflecting their hearts in her brown eyes.

Her imagination influenced and navigated
towards a rejuvenating feeling,
When she goes swimming and day dreaming in naturally
welcoming cold and cool water springs.

While helplessly day dreaming,
Her heart drifted away and spoke of a hidden splendour,
While listening to the breeze and the breathing of
Corsican Pine trees,
While listening to old songs speaking to the soul,
On an old tape recorder.
While waiting in anticipation
For the fragrant-filled air of home-made cakes,
As they rises inside the oven.

Reveries formed,
With the never-ending rapturous moments,
From the sights, smells, sounds, tastes and touches of
reality.
Creative emotional juice runs through her imagination,
Like Stallions on rich meadow pastures.
While at dawn,
She found the presence of hope,
Hovering in the silence.

The balance of life hangs upon,
The embellishments of these small moments,
These embellishments performed together,
Engraved inside the heart of a passionate writer.

7. Seasoned Verse in Autumn Colours

Instead of salt, pepper and spices,
A well-seasoned verse is prepared
With emotions we feel strongly about.

Like tailoring a rather rich home-made beauty,
A traditional scrapbook of verses and phrases,
Photographs and embellishments,
Personalised stickers and ribbons,
Crooked and oddly-shaped buttons,
Attractive fabric and decorative paper,
Memorabilia of times spent together.

Of hand-made paper daffodils,
Fabricating their timeline inside my journal;
Holding on to dear life for the arrival of Autumn,
To mingle,
To associate with ripe coloured passionate leaves,
Firmly attached, inside the pages.
The Daffodils stayed,
They stayed, even when Spring has passed away.
They lived past April, unharmed.
Still favourable to my sight, if not my other senses.

Finding truth in the seasons of a man's life,
Rather than,
The seasons of a year;
Seasons of whys,hows and what ifs.
Seasons of strength, weaknesses and ordinary miracles.

One autumn afternoon,
Standing on my bedroom balcony,
The warm soothing wind brings me,
Written leaves of mustard yellow hues,
Freeing them from being tied down to one obvious
colour.
Unlike written letters,
These written autumn leaves,
Ignites my emotions and sets my heart on fire.

The fall season has many untold stories,
But mine are not left untold,
They are merely hidden, away from plain sight,
Buried for now, like a time capsule.
For on that inevitable day,
Your selfless soul will finally unearth them.

Among the fall foliage,
A fiery-red coloured leave is ready,
Ready to write a letter for poets and lovers;
Where it landed, will decide its destiny.

Its final home could be -
The pavement grey,
Where empty feet would mindlessly step upon it,
Ignorant of its beauty, denying any attachment.
Or it could end up inside the pages,
The precious pages of a scrapbook lover,
Cherishing its existence,
Of how once it hung on top of a majestic tree,
Witnessing real impressionable love stories.

And ah! a well-seasoned verse is sometimes,
Conceived under the Corsican Pine trees of Meghalaya,
On my nature-walks,
The Pine trees offer a therapeutic scent,
Much needed inside my head,
To revive that underlying creative feeling.
The Pine needles too,
Those fallen and those on top of the tree,
Are showcasing a smooth carpet of art,
For the sun and the blue sky to see.

But finally, one must admit,
The noble beauty of the Pine cones,
Collected, they hugged the human palm,
Modified a little in artistic hands,
They now found a new home.

The naturally crafted ornamental objects,
They are a creative expression all on their own.

24

8. Appreciation of the Dandelion Wildflower while Dancing a Waltz Around its Citrus and Rose Fragrant Notes

I am a Dandelion seed dancing in the wind,
Circling the fingers that plucked me.
I waited to be picked by unhurried strangers,
A chance for me to change their day entirely.

I despise the birds feeding on me hastily,
But I love adorning in nectar and pollen,
I love wearing a necklace made of dewdrops,
For the butterflies and the bees.
But what I love the most is,
When human hands need not intervene,
Their hands need not tend to my needs.
I exist on my own
For the purpose of praising the ability of my maker.

A note to self to be prepared,
To stand attractively,

For when you have the need to pluck me.

I preferred the unhurried slender fingers
Of a young girl with a gleeful heart,
A young girl's mindset -
Not yet diluted by deceptions,
Not yet filtered by obligations.
Young innocent girls pluck to praise me
And not to erase me.

While the mindset of middle-aged ladies
Are now conformed to modernity,
Unquestioned by humanity;
I am an uninvited guest
On their manicured lawns and their exclusive flower
beds,
When I grow there, they think of me,
An invader of social structure.

Some perceived me and my family -
Some perceived me to be an undesirable weed.
Of an unwanted kind,
As if to suffocate my flora friends with leisure.
So I must go where I am appreciated and approved.

So away from gardens I must go,
I will thrive on the sides of the roads,

On that dearest cracked pavement's chest,
I will have new beginnings on unconfined sidewalks.
Standing unafraid of human feet
Walking aggressively towards me.

Strengthening my roots,
Now a resident of the crevices.
However,
No human can ignore my vibrant personality,
Just when I thought I belonged on dusty old pavements,
Someone came along to recognise me.

Despite my stubborn nature,
Someone is inclined to pick me.
So I ended up a boutonnière
On some young lad's front pocket.
When he took me home and forgot about me,
I faltered away on his rustic wooden dresser,
Until the sympathetic wind would come and take me,
Taking me away and giving me a proper burial.

Outside the young lad's garden I can feel the earth
starting its chore of covering my withered bones.

The earth covered me like a warm blanket,
I have now woken up from a deep slumber to wonder,
To overcome new challenges and challenge adversity

itself.
I am known for my resilience,
Yes! I am resilient in nature.
I am able to stay alive in the harshest conditions known
to man.

I have an urgent need to go on an adventure,
My fearless self craves to exist and express,
I desire only to embrace and explore;
I cannot resist the call of an adventure.

I know what has to be done,
Even if I haven't done it before.
I want to be swaddled in the arms of the wind,
"Please carry me to the other side of the hedge."
I eagerly whispered a soft prayer.

I want poems written about joyous moments of
Dandelion seeds breaking in the air,
Waiting for some kind human to say,
"I blew its white puff today."
Experiencing a change of scenery,
Dandelion seeds breaking in the air,
Breaking into a secret song,
Among the clouds and the leaves,
Among the restless ants
Keeping busy on the branches of a tree.

Me and my siblings sang a song and painted the
atmosphere,
Unheard by human ears and unseen by human eyes.
We float far away, gently above the ocean,
Watching seashells washed upon the shore,
Exposing their beautiful form innocently.

We dance elegantly in our white chiffon dresses and
gowns,
So painlessly, with no incapability;
Underneath the perfectly moonlit sky,
Letting the wind decide where to take us,
Always residing somewhere safe,
Even when we have been floating through the chaos.

We could land near a farm house on the hill
Or settled on the warm ground near the mill,
Or stayed until the Spring could watch us sprout near
the ferns and the snails.

My fluffy head seed likes to travel, now you know.
To live a life of unexpected circumstance;
Oh! the joy of living an undisturbed life.

You see, my clocks fight a different kind of battle,
To safeguard the adventures of life.

Oh human, in sincerity I know,
During my prime I am edible,
But as an elder I profusely begged,
To reconsider lengthening my lifespan,

Before I reach old age and retire,
I have a desire to live my life to the fullest.
I have heard of legends from your forefathers,
Legends of traditional hands nurturing me and collecting
me.
Because I am edible and powerful in my entirety.

But, if only you knew,
Of why I wanted to stay alive much longer,
Let me tell you of a way to set up a plan,
A plan to realise I matter,
I want to matter,
To live the fondest parts of my life,
So let me be,
Let me live for carefree hearts,
Of those unbothered lovers.

I envisioned my vibrant yellow flower head
With my hollow stem
Embracing the hair of a beautiful young woman.
My multiple ray petite florets
Posing as a worthy accessory,

An ornamental bloom of steadfast loyalty.

Yes, If I must die,
I would like to have died a dignified death.
What could be more dignified than to have been worn on
a graceful warrior's head?
A warrior who fought for her perfect love.
She told me of how she fell in love as her man
ran his fingers through her hazel-nut brown hair.

Oh human, I love to go on adventures,
To live a full life that satisfies my curiosity.
But on the other hand,
Today, I must stop to think about myself,
Today, I have returned, to serve you differently.
I must think of someone else,
To think about humans, anyone, other than myself.

I have an urge to share a secret with you,
I am created to fight another kind of battle.
Now it is my turn to serve you in ways so divine,
I have the ability to heal you if you allow me,
I will spare my time, but you need not spare my life.

I may be frail on the outside
But I am a weapon in disguise,
A nutritional powerhouse.

I am fully armoured,
From the top of my flower head,
To my midrib, to the tip of my roots.
My petals can be coated in flour, egg and milk batter,
to fry with some olive oil and ginger.
My petals can also be baked to sit on a cupcake,
My petals can also be boiled for syrups and jams.

My bracts, along with my lamina and my leaf can
accompany salads on elegant dinner trays.

Nutrients runs through my body and my veins,
I could be a tonic,
An antioxidant to assist a fellow warrior - the Liver,
An organ of perseverance,
An organ who wage wars,
Making sure, checking and patrolling,
For ailments and conditions of the human body.

Along with the Liver we can detoxify and cleanse.
I am a friend, a dietary supplement,
For digestive issues and threatening heart burns,
For plagues and undervalued headaches,
For unnecessary swelling and unkind kidney diseases.

My roots can engaged in long conversations
With a slice of lemon inside porcelain teapots,

On a journey to enhance that perfectly hot cup of tea.
And my finely cut and boiled Dandelion roots can swim
inside the glasses of refreshing beverages,
Mixed and mastered with delicious Valencia Oranges.

Having found the flavour of life itself,
Now, I can die a dignified death.
To die in a dignified manner,
we must learn to serve another.
I adapted, I transformed as I am resilient in nature.

Created to serve, created to be needed.
Reminded me of a King who once came,
Not to be served, but to serve.
If only humankind would learn to love to serve one
another, with humility and grace, expecting nothing in
return,
Then humankind would know peace and purpose of a far
greater nature.

9. The Beauty of Enhanced Frozen Water Crystals - More about Plot Twists and Loop Holes and Golden Dewdrop Hedges

From afar,
A snowflake may appear unremarkable,
But up close,
The details of an ice crystal would leave one speechless.

The enhanced structure of a Snowflake,
Each one a rare find, each kind of rare design.

Holding secrets,
Incomprehensible to the human mind.
With its irregular shape so refine,
Arranged like a battle plan,
Melting away at the touch of a man's hand.

Like snowflakes and movies,
The former declaring their Uniqueness,
And the latter,

Anchored in Loop Holes and Plot Twists.
So also,
Each woman's heart is never of the same kind,
Each one so uniquely formed,
Each one having Loop holes,
Each one with unexpected Plot Twists and Turns.

A woman's heart has endless winding paths,
Multiple features of mazes and puzzles,
Golden Dewdrop and Skyflower hedges,
Cautionary seeds sowed around the edges,
Gracefulness and refinement radiates,
Within the fibres of her being.
Intimidating, yet, captivating,
Sometimes rewarding,
If the gaze is manoeuvred by a courageous man.

Their hearts have been somersaulting,
Through a series of plot twists from real-life drama.
Their minds floating around the idea of love,
But most times encountering fictional romance;
All this frivolity and unpredictability, automatically,
Switch their hearts into a suspense thriller mode.

The way to a woman's heart,
Truth be told, is a complicated matter,
However,

Loopholes exists for knights in shining armour.
Loyalty is the only exceptional way,
For those who care,
To keep a woman of grace from wavering away.

Men of integrity tend to hold accountability
For their actions in every unplanned direction.
Their genuine generosity and child-like availability
Revealed the details of a woman's heart,
Never aloud but always in a subtle manner.

The gravity of faith pulls love to the centre,
The centre of her happily ever after.
Though the way to a woman's life demands creativity,
The way to her eyes is simply knowing the details of her
heart .

When analysed closely,
The heart of a woman is like a beautiful snowflake,
Her heart is a spectacular ice crystal.
And when a man of value would take the time,
To study her,
To look beyond her accomplishments,
Under the microscope of his love for her,
There, the details of her heart will be revealed,
The details, the jewels to his crown;
Which he will later on 'Wear',

With her by his side, a soulmate supporter,
Forever entwined.

10. Breathing with the Stars while Singing with the Garden Phlox

Cast your dark brown beautiful eyes at the dark night
sky,
The moon seems to have lost its way tonight,
Just as a lonesome traveller is trying to find her way
home tonight,
To sing a song of mourning for the great Lawson
Cypress Pine Tree;
To find a way out of the wilderness and into the light.

The Garden Phlox sang this song, in my mind,
"Will you breathe with the stars again?
To breathe in the memories of your grandfather's stories,
Of climbing Plum trees and being carefree.
Breathe, while the maker hears the longing of your soul.
Breathe, to unveil a long lost more established self,
Breathe, to bring back that forgotten essence,
An essence unattainable by most."

The Garden Phlox of various shades,
Of Lavender, Lilac, Pink and Salmon colour
spoke to me through paper;

But the White and Purple colour calls me
from outside my window,
To breathe in its long-lasting scent
of a purpose driven nature.

The Garden Phlox is breathing with the stars,
Its tall stature, giving it the ability to see me.
It hears the sound of my voice amidst the noise,
It hears a song of unshed tears under my heavily-veiled
human chest.

The Garden Phlox has stood there,
Beautifying my front yard since 1999,
The great Lawson Cypress Pine trees,
Planted when I was born, in 1991,
Grew stronger each year,
Sheltering the Phlox from above.

Having thoughts of friendship,
Of harmonious coexistence,
The Phlox continually,
Recalled and replayed memories of
The two Lawson Cypress Pine trees,
Graciously fragrant, providing a safe abode,
For brilliant birds with melodies.

Oh, how it broke my human heart,

On the day they had to be cut down.
Just to make way for cold lifeless cement,
Of trivial meaning, to live eternally.
On the ground the branches fell,
A sad gush of wind in my hair;
I reached for the miniature beautiful cones,
Holding them on the palm of my hand,
Forever separated from the fallen tree.
An evergreen,
Undefeated by Winter
But amputated by mere human hands.

A wreath of Garden Phlox hangs on the tree stumps
from time to time,
To honor the memory of these great trees.
Even though
Each tree was being cut down differently,
The pain was always the same.
One tree fell and then the other,
The pain stayed on for many years,
Each tree felt my overwhelming tears.

Takotsubo cardiomyopathy occured
When the Lawson Cypress fell,
A series of powerlessness to breathe happened,
After that traumatic event.
The Garden Phlox send a gesture of will power,

By swaying and pushing out
its dense cluster of bright dainty flowers.
Exhaling a sweet scent that spoke,
Of its promising characteristics,
Of shared feelings and united earthy matter.

The Panicles of pure innocence,
Spiritual wisdom and faithfulness,
Fall elegantly on their own,
On the grass, near my toes,
Now a garland fixed on my head,
My mind furnished with these qualities.

The Garden Phlox breathe life into the inanimate
painting on the Canvas of my heart,
Painting a garland of trust and togetherness,
A collage of forgotten dreams,
Paving a way for emotional artistry.

11. Battle Scars of the Human Mind -Echoes From the Deserted Mountains of the Subconscious Mind

The thorns of depression slowed me down,
The thistles of anxiety bruised my mind.
The thorns and thistles have turned me,
Reflecting unrecognised pain in my eyes.

Living in a world of dissociation and disconnection,
The thorns interfered with the lovely-lively soul,
While the thistles overwhelmingly scarred my reality.
Henceforth,
A chainmail of thorns and thistles I will create,
A coat of armour, a hauberk of fiery temperament,
I will wear them and share them to defend myself.
A chainmail of defense mechanism to shield me.

Disruption to emotional order from familiar faces and
places,
Unwanted near the green pastures,
Unfamiliar by Violets near the Water Springs;
On dehydrated land, I stand, unwanted.

So,I will be the Prickly Pear Cactus plant,
A survivalist of the rarest kind;
Stranded in the wilderness of life,
Prepared for battles in the deserts highway,
Standing in a vast desert of inevitable sandstorms.

As years pass by, I stayed vigilant,
My hideaways restricted to desolated, deserted regions.
Concealing over anxious thoughts of over complicated
matters.
Woven by the cords of sand, rocks and rainless skies.

Teenage years nurtured in the driest examples,
Of dull strangers with treacherous minds.
I developed a mask,
Parading around in my sharp spines to instill fear,
So that poisonous eyes and criticising tongues will
neither shake me nor break me.

Sharpened and Stretched out to tackle hurtful critics
from flying towards me.
While over anxious judgemental eyes says,
"She prick us and pierce us."
A splinter on their cowardly flesh,
Their skin so thick, I was inflicted.

The vultures never saw my true nature,
The leaves of a good heart.
I stand beneath the burning sun,
An ignorant observer.
The flowing stream nowhere near me,
I have prepared to foresee a potential injury,
I caused a series of allergic reactions to an enemy in the
guise of a friend or family.

I am a warrior, I will not falter,I will not faint.
A unique adaptation will I discover from within my
veins.
In response to the harsh waves of societal expectations,
I will thrive unafraid,
I will wear sharp spines on my arms and my knees,
Defending against hunters and gatherers,
Who were trained to destroy me.

Living inside a psychological thriller,
Of shameless spectators,
Here, I waited, my sharp spines favourably intact,
Fearless tears absorbed, to water a hidden beauty.

Raising budding flowers hidden within me,
Floral buds knitted and formed,
When I was still in my mother's womb.
These blossoms inborn,

Always wanted to stay internally,
Inborn anti-inflammatory properties,
Which can help and heal in plenty.

Here, my true purpose intertwined with my battle scars,
Must I hide my vibrant gifted flavour?
The Prickly Pear does not hide those exceptionally
beautiful flowers.
The softest yellow, so kind to human eyes.

A prayer warrior goes to fight her battles in the spiritual
realm,
Softly the truth embraced her and she becomes
strengthened.

The unsuspected consciousness regains its anointed robe,
And softer still in this manner,
The anointing hand transformed a fellow warrior;
My battle scars are meant to pave a way,
A way for wearied, younger, prayer warriors.

To let Him who speak order, take over,
Take over the chaos, take over the fight.
The spiritually vigilant becomes beautifully
unrecognised as we stand in His light.

So my story goes,

One fine day,
The humidity led the healing rain towards me,
Clouds formed above me,
Raining and absorbing my desert away.
The water ran to the deepest veins of my body;
Though not frequently,
The rain came and washed my pain away.

The one who makes me, oh, so wise,
He purifies the prayer warrior's heart during the struggle
and the fight;
Unbeknownst to me,
He held my hand,
He held me.
I am a succulent Prickly Pear,
My potentialities are hidden within,
My wounded skin,
Still unbroken, still alive,
Dancing in this battlefield called life.

Endangered and of the Old fashioned kind,
We are both endangered species,
The Prickly Pear and I.
At risk of extinction,
Witnessing the loss of our habitat from change of human
conditions.

Delicate part of the human heart,
A Prickly Pear Cactus flower,
A captivating beauty,
See the innocence in a world of pain.

The surrendered past can no longer cast,
A fearful, loveless heart.
In time, a juicy red fruit is reproduced,
Emerged from within the Prickly Pear.
We have the ability to love and bear fruit,
No matter the rough exterior.
If all we have is a shattered past,
The re-invention of a flawless weapon
Will lead us forward without hesitation.
This weapon is not of this world,
A weapon forged by Love itself.

P.S. - When you have learned to surrender yourself to
the love within you,
Here, your battles are won.

A love free from self-doubt and self-condemnation,
A love with no records of the pain you went through.

Footnotes - My spines and needles are metaphors,
Of habits unaccepted in social get togethers.
My spines and needles are also an armour,

A protective covering.

My philosophy of choosing love over worldly wealth and power,

Was not a wise way of life for the modern thinker.

12. The Bombarded Heart of a Writer

A Writer writes when heartbreak hits her,
Battling a broken heart,
Fighting to live,
Super active,
Still being vigilant and awake,
A battle so severe,
A war of the mind,
Fought by humankind,
From time to time.

A Writer doesn't desire comfort food,
To numb her pain,
A Writer doesn't want to join a club,
To anesthetize her shame.

she wants to encounter, to talk to,
The wounded parts of herself,
She wants to embrace the throbbing pain,
She wants to embrace the feeling of sadness,
While struggling through unfavorable waters,
Unprepared.

She hears music in the thunderstorm,

Yesterday she walked with the rain,
She feels refresh, she is reborn.
Whenever devastation accurately strikes her,
A new poem is born,
A new story is under construction.

Give someone a White Rose,
It will just be a forgotten flower,
Give a creative soul a White Rose,
And it will turn out to be,
A Souvenir of those loss hours.

My heart is being bombarded,
But I will not speak of those attacks,
Instead, I want to write about,
The beauty of nature,
Alongside,
The beauty of my mother.

The earth is nurturing wild seeds,
Dropped by purposeful birds,
Travelling on their life's journey.
I am nurturing sweet-peas,
The sweet-pea knows the lines on my fingers,
I am waiting for them to blossom and retain,
The scent, which eases my brain,
For I am an overthinker.

The bees and the butterflies came,
They came not merely for the beautiful appearances.
But to gather the sweetest nectar,
Waiting underneath the alluring postures,
Of the attractive exterior.

The Pomegranate tree of lost times,
Stayed in an old photograph album,
Immortalised with my mortal self.
But the Pomegranate tree loss its life,
A photo captured, when I was seven.

Wild Tiger Lilies and Wild Apricot Vine,
Grew happily on our front yard,
Untamed but never unwanted,
Never unkind.

Primroses and Yellow Tiger Lilies,
My mother's favourite flowers,
A beautiful smile on her face, came by,
Unannounced, yet, much desired.
Oh, the lovely Spring afternoons!
If she could get a chance,
To prune and plant,
Her favourite flowers.
I would hear a happy hint in her voice,

A personality filled with unconditional love,
My mother.
I love the hum, that gentle tune, the hymn,
She had acquired.
A beautiful soul, so kind and rare,
Makes the life of the wounded,
Still worth living,
Most of us, reconstructed and repaired.

Beds of Chrysanthemum,
Of various colours,
Grew together,
A picture of my mother,
Still young, planting flowers in my mind.

She found new strength in solitude,
When faced with a heart-wrenching reality;
She found healing on a path,
Where others might have been utterly more broken.

Agonising circumstances fueled her goals,
The song, "Blessed Assurance",
A theme song for her role.
A lady of her kind,
Manufactured purpose and hope,
Even when the traumatic past slyly tried to blind her.

13. The Tapestry of An Adventurer Who Dream of Passion-Flowers

The hand that holds the thread and the wool,
Produces a stitching of the most beautiful
Passion-flowers.
Standing in a meadow of old dreams,
A meadow of different colours,
A dramatic show, an eye-catching factor.
The tapestry wool and the needle-threader,
Tools for an insightful tapestry maker.

The tapestry came to be,
A combination of life-giving character,
Of Passion-flowers set in June till September.
Matured Vines and beautifully shaped leaves
Weaved with colours of dark green and ember.

And two human forms weaved in perfection,
A man and a woman, in love, as they require,
Kept holding hands near a romantically lid fire.
This tapestry was filled with real-life memories,
Of young love in summer.

The Bearded Irises of pastel coloured threads,
Ran across the borders;
Then, on the center of this heavy cloth,
A Castaneous coloured Squirrel,
Like a rich Chestnut,
Ran around the Pomelo trees,
Escaping with a Pomelo tree flower,
Indifferent to human existence.

One day we will hang our tapestries,
For wonderful curious eyes to see;
With threads of vibrant colours,
Shedding a light of hope,
On our particular patterns of living.
Of decorative designs interlocking,
To create a chain reaction of our thoughts intervening.

On the other side of the tapestry,
Aslan, the Lion, stands in command,
A Shepherd that maketh the wolves tremble.
His sheep rejoice, for they know His voice,
Amidst the powerless shadows and figures.

An overflow cup and a well-set table,
Set aside for the sheep with anointed wool.
A gesture of love for green pastures and still waters,
A tapestry filled with Narnian theme and colours.

A series of accurate needle-work and patience,
Others call it Needlepoint or Canvas work in action.
For those sinking in the quick sand of unimaginable
monotonous living,
They finally chose to divert their thoughts in tapestry
making.

A fabric that transcends the boundaries of society,
Secret experiences of an adventurer told on a tapestry.
A tapestry of simple living and peaceful home-making,
Detached from material faults and faking.

A hand-woven timeless tapestry,
Showcasing the way you live and the way you give,
Allowing the properly selected tapestry wool,
To wander and to cater,
Allowing the wool of your choice,
To define you.
The colourful threads which aspires to amuse you,
Wrap the finished product of designs,
That sings to the rhythm of your fingers.

If your life is like a tapestry,
If the way you love is like embroidery,
What kind of thread would define your mind set?
To let the gift to communicate finally find you.

14. Bethlehem Lily - Unspoken Soul Ties

A recollection of the fine scent,
Subconsciously relevant to a poet,
A fragrance so mysteriously emotional,
Triggered my olfactory memory.

The Bethlehem Lily,
A visitor of the quiet night,
A species of cactus kind,
A white-petaled Lily flower,
A blessing for the human mind.

The fragrance so wonderfully intense,
Gave me an electrical feeling,
Highly exciting,
Of having travelled back in time.

The mind transported,
Triggered and time travelled,
Unlocking explicit memories of unspoken soul ties,
Focused on those fluttering stomach butterflies.

The sentimental night,
Could sense my beating heart,

A heart rushing and speeding,
Within me, within my petrified unspoken past,
Prevailing to unleash the restrained passion.

A rare jem,which will rarely bloom,
But when it does, it's like the arrival of royalty.
The fragrance can soothe a lonely soul,
A fragrance so heavenly,
It frees conditions of chained morbidity.

The fragrance tell its own story,
As the white petals open gently,
In a refined majestic manner,
When the night comes to a halt.

My mother and I,
Always talked about,
The unforgettable scent,
Today, still thriving in our lives.

The flower dances only in the moonlight,
A plant from an honourable clan,
A royalty in the midst of commoners,
Pure sight, pure delight, made me teary eyed.

Its scent gives life to the hours of the night,
Reduces mental and respiratory catastrophe,

Evoking strong sentimental flashbacks,
Personal touches of previous memories.

The Bethlehem Lily opens dramatically,
Revealing a "trough" or "crib" shape inside,
Rekindling the thought of sacred celebration,
A representation of the birth of Jesus Christ,
A central event in Christian faith and tradition.

Bethlehem's role, in history,
Often foretold, of a great story,
That Jesus was born in Bethlehem,
A town in Judea.

The manger and the star,
Symbolises the beginning of Jesus' life.
In humility and simplicity,
He came to serve, to revive human lives.

Revived, in the middle of the dark,
The stars parted the clouds,
To gaze at this beautiful creation,
Thrived and stayed alive before human eyes.

Within the chamber of the Bethlehem Lily,
A sense of comfort externalised,
Deep spiritual connection arise,

Once you breathe in,

The individually distinctive scent,

You will see eye to eye with Carpe diem.

15. The Passiflora Incarnata of the Beloved Lavender Colour

AND

The Passiflora Caerulea of White Clouds and Blue Skies Weather

Part - 1

I had the privilege to nurture a living treasure,
A flora friend flourishing in my garden.
The Passion-fruit vine climbed the wooden trellis,
A particular kind, the purple Passiflora Incarnata.
Oh beautiful flower,
Oh Passiflora Incarnata,
Your properties can wash away anxiety and insomnia.

Against my garden wall or near the sheltered shed,
Away from damaging winds of harsh weather.
Now, an established beauty for hearts on fire,

Climbing ahead and around an arching structure.

Of all the Passion-flowers,
The White Passiflora Caerulea,
With its Blue-crown of royal origin,
Blooms a little better.

Its beauty spoke to my mind,
My eyes can no longer
Just look at a picture,
Now in need of gazing
At the real-petal flower.

Then here and now,
This invasive Vine started to invade,
The organic kitchen garden started to fade.
But, I didn't mind! For who can duplicate?
The beautiful Passion-flower,
With its heart-awakening fruit.
The Yellowish-Orange glossy looking fruit,
Ripening to bloom and to wonder,
Having a picture-perfect natural amber colour.

In early spring the fertilizer fed the Passion-flower,
Then the Honey bees and the Carpenter bees received an
extended invitation from nature.
They started their journey without retire,

They arrived in style,
Buzzing like a properly rehearsed choir,
To meet their pleasant host with pleasure.

Wired to have an attraction to Passion flowers,
The bees came for the nectar and the pollen,
And for warm home-made days to remember;
The Passiflora, a food source from nature.

Detailed landing pads,
Thought about by the creator,
An attraction for bees to dance and then to gather;
Especially the Honey bee with its yellow Chamomile colour,
Dancing away until they returned home in December.

Part - 2

The Passion-flower resided near the countryside,
Near cottages of expert and amateur gardeners.
A beautiful flower and a delightful fruit,
Perceived to contain a prophetic calling,
Hence, enriched the faith of all believers.

Passion-flowers exhibit an open structure,
White filaments and powdery anthers,
Standing together in unison.

At the center of the flower head,
A stigma protrudes,
A signification of heart-pounding wonder.

The Passion-flower,
Particularly the Passiflora Caerulea,
Its various parts, in human hearts, we know,
Represents the different elements,
Of the most life-changing event.

Christian missionaries gave the vine
"Passion Fruit" its name,
When they opened their eyes and analysed,
That parts of the flower spoke of the good news,
It resembled the anointed Christian message,
Specifically the resurrection of Jesus Christ.

Often perceived as a symbol,
A blessed illustration,
Of Jesus' scourging,
Of His sacrificial love.
Of how He gave His life,
On His own accord, of course.
Of why He worn the crown of thorns,
The shame he took without a pause.

With pierced hands and feet,

Read this, as a reminder,
In agony, He was nailed to the cross,
His face bruised, with bones exposed,
His face, no longer recognised.
It was for us He suffered there,
The unknown pain He had to bear,
His never-ending thirst.

Oh, to comprehend the love,
The "Passion of Christ,"
He paid the price,
The debt removed,
Our wages are forgiven.
A Lamb so pure,
A Lamb of high value hierarchical order,
His heart was broken for human brokenness,
A sacrificial Lamb,
Who knew no blemish nor imperfection,
A sacrificial Lamb,
The reigning King, the living One, the resurrected Son.

Our complicated lives,
He simplified,
So we might live beyond death, into forever.
And when He died, He conquered death,
In Glorified form, He went home to His Father.
Left behind an empty tomb,

For us to humbly remember,
The dictatorship of fears and tears,
Now ashes in dying fire.

That guilt-ridden part of our hearts,
That burdened age, suddenly, finally over.
Rest assured, He hears your prayer,
He listened, so you must listen too!
Listen to the still soft voice,
Stay away from worldly noise;
There's a healer for faltered hearts,
Walk with Him, walk in pure gentleness.
A counsellor of Holiness,
From now on into forever.

Part - 3

Let us hear the message from the Passion-flower itself:

"I am the Passion-flower",
The picture of "Suffering" and "Resurrection",
The Latin word "Passio," fits my fame,
They observe these on my frame.
The Passion of Christ,
Who conquered debt and conquered death,
Till His last breath, until He said, "It is finished".

My classic petals and valuable sepals,
Are interpreted to be the ten faithful apostles,
With the exclusion of the other two.
In history we're told, only one returned,
The only one who walked with Him on water.

My crown-like structure,
The Blue-crown Passion-flower,
Specifically, the Passiflora Caerulea,
Are seen as the crown of thorns on His anointed head.

And oh, the spiraled tendrils,
The coiling tendrils,
Tendrils of the flower fair,
The thread-like plant organ,
Are the whips used in the flagellation of Christ.
The flogging of flawless life,
The lash, the beating instrument of old times.

The slender stalk connected to my stigma,
My tall, vertical, slim feature,
The pollen-receiving part,
Are called the styles.
They are fashioned like iron nails,
The seven to nine inches kind;
Which pierced and impaled,
His loving hands and gentle feet.

The three stigmas on top of my styles,
They look like the famous nail heads,
Those notorious nail heads,
Like square-shaped iron,
Attached to my slender styles.
Used in crucifixion, to hold the palms,
To hold them to the wooden cross.

One of my stigma also represents,
More than the obvious things above,
It takes the shape and structure of,
The sponge, the absorbent object,
Not forgotten by those involved.

Drenched in blood,
Drenched in sweat,
His brain and body bathe in pain;
There, somewhere near,
The vessel full of sour wine,
The only thing for His thirst,
The non-soothing kind.

The vinegar that touched the dying hour,
The sponge soaked and steeped in bitter water,
The sour wine that touched His final breath,
Witnessed the Lamb of God with

Parched throat and throbbing pain,
Overexertion and muscle strain,
Overly heightened excruciating pain.

The sour wine on the sponge,
Atop the hyssop stalk,
Could it be ?
A crude short-lived pain reliever,
Or a form of shameless mockery,
Or to make the chastisement clearer,
Or to make Him conscious of the pain,
To prolong the merciless suffering,
Or could it be to moisten his throat,
Allowing Him to say those final three words.

My stamens and my anthers fair,
Candidly appears to be,
The wounded parts, the battered bits,
The wounds that left a resounding scar,
On the body of the King of Kings,
A king who plastered a repentant heart,
The day after.

My three-lobed leaf with its pointed tips,
Reminded mankind of the chosen spear,
The shape of the Holy Lance in display,
A Christian relic of the world today.

The last tearful act to ensure He died,
The awful spear that pierced Jesus' side.

Passion-flowers with white and blue hues,
The Passiflora Caerulea,
Of White Clouds colour and Blue Skies weather,
These are the colours of my personal preference,
The colours I chose when I look at the flower.
So, don't misunderstand them for the official definition,
Of the Passiflora Caerulea.

The Passiflora Caerulea,
Makes me stay in seasons of White Clouds and
Blue Skies weather,
My visualization begins to breathe again;
The Passiflora Caerulea,
Often interpreted in the past and in times to come,
A symbol of the Heavenly Kingdom,
So meaningfully pure forever after.

The Fragrance of the Passion-flower signifies,
The spices the women brought to the tomb,
A perfume made for Jesus;
In remembrance of His Sacrifice,
Intended to honor the body of Christ,
An act of embalming,
A fragrance representing precious life.

He took my burden on His shoulders,
My penalty, He paid in full,
He held my hand and led me,
On a path of sanctification,
With love and not with rules.

Footnotes -

John 19:39 - "Nicodemus also, who earlier had come to Jesus by night, came bringing a mixture of myrrh and aloes, about seventy-five pounds in weight."

16. Be a Walnut Shell in a World of Ice-Cream Flavours

It is quite alright to be different,
To be amongst the marginalised group of thinkers,
To be a walnut shell,
To be the solid Coffee-coloured protective layer.
Be a shell that encloses and hides your kernel,
Not easily accessible by powerful influencers,
Your mission is to safekeep,
To redefine your own kind.

The world will try to reach your heart,
The world will try to infect your kernel,
Those you meet will try to indirectly teach you,
With their glances of immature thoughts,
With their branded clothes and strange words,
Those assumptions and smirks,
Those cold-hearted eyes and bitter statements,
They contaminated, judged and painted our image
without redemption.

But you cannot adapt to the ways of the world,
No matter how hard they try to crush your shell,

No matter how determined their hammer is,
Your beautiful Kernel will still be shielded,
Your beautiful heart will matter one day.

In a world of facade and double standard,
You will never find your true self,
If you allow them to tame you.
If you follow the ways of this world,
You'll have to compromise,
Until there's nothing left of you.
You could live unsatisfactorily
Making sacrifices and living selflessly,
Just to find a Watered-down version of 'You'.
Your unique personality locked away,
Under masks of a stranger's persona,
Just to fit in, in a dark reality.
Just to have a short-lived love,
Just to have acceptance,
Drowning in a society of pretenses,
And harmful inescapable appearances.

One's Originality is your identity,
A blessed God-given personality,
That was never meant to be hidden,
Under filters and beauty applications.
Be quirky of the original kind,
Be human but keep in mind,

Your affectionate side and your flawless eyes,
Should only be read by your life partner.
Your hidden spark can grow stronger still,
Nurtured in the hands of your trusted man.
Fight for the voiceless,
Fight to be free from the complex of inferiority.

If people cannot accept
Your way of thinking ahead,
Be 'Different' on your own,
Be better at standing out,
Yes! Stand out, Stand strong, Stand alone,
Rather than fit in and lose yourself.

You can contribute so much to the world,
Like a Walnut Shell, You can help remove,
The unwanted faded paint of social injustices,
The rust that eats away the kind-hearted ones,
The life-threatening contaminants;
You could help sort out a messy pile of unhappiness,
From the surface of people's lives,
To later help them stand in better soil,
To help them prune and see them through,
Without damage for them and nothing untrue.

But we live in a world where people will Use us,
They will choose us as their mobility aid,

For their broken heart, foot and ankle.
We can be their Crutches and Knee Scooters,
But once they can stand and walk again,
They will downright neglect us.
Take a chance to replace us,
Then heartlessly update us,
They will silently destroy us.
So, there's a different route, for those among us,
Who wants to preserve our colourful hues,
Better to have just one friend, a trusted life partner,
Rather than to have a roomful of friends,
Who never really knew you.
Who knew not how to know you.

I am a Walnut Shell, I am impenetrably whole,
My Kernel heart reserved for a few good people.
I would rather have a colourful peaceful life,
Away from social interactions,
Away from vain attempts,
Away from cunning wealth and competitions.
I would instead write poetry
and traditional love letters,
Be passionate about glass painting
and pressing petal flowers,
Walk in the Word of God,
Walk in wisdom and in love.
Read a book, for long hours,

Undisturbed, near a window,
Re-enacting the journey of Mayflowers,
Magnolia trees and flowers.
Collect real letters of pens and papers,
Take photographs of little moments,
Bake an Apple Cake, bake some Scones and after,
Plant a seed, plant a flower,
A Sapling of my own.
Take long nature-walks with my man,
Fall in love with him again and again,
Fall in love with gratitude in my palm,
When he held my hand and told me,
'Your beauty is unfading, unaffected and untamed,
Nurturing a realistically brainstorming brain,
Underneath that classic Walnut Shell!'

17. Deep Reflective Thoughts of Someone Born in 1991

If you were born in 1991,
Old school ideas and the content way of life
Begins to move in an unwavering motion,
Inside your mind, with your strength,
Those contemplating thoughts begin
To have an open-ended interpretation.

Here lies a treasure that wealth cannot bind,
A time when our lives were not yet inclined,
Towards smartphones and social media dilemma.
When technology has not yet occupied the mind;
We had freedom of unbiased thoughts,
Accompanied by uninfluenced emotions.

Souvenirs which can be held in our hand,
Real keep sakes which can be handed down,
Of home-made items created and invented,
With effortless love of the thoughtfully talented,
Items of meaningful discovery of the self.

Days of photo albums and traditional love letters;

Photos that lived on the gallery of our homes and never
on the gallery of our phones.
A photo of a loved one kept inside a wallet,
Or safely hangs inside a locket, so elegantly,
Adorning a young woman's swan-like neck.

A time when a gentleman would write,
A proper love letter with ink pens and real paper.
Landline were a definite invasion of privacy,
A landmine of inappropriate whispered rumours.
Cell phones were extravagant accessories,
Not on the range of affordability for many.
So, handwritten letters spoke louder,
Specifically to a writer and a lover.

Love letters sometimes witnessed,
A tragedy of complicated duplicity,
The deceitfulness written in paper,
Which later dance in the fireplace.

But Love letters of pure faithfulness,
Those of true love and sacrifices,
Stayed safe inside wooden dressers,
Between books and in old canvas suitcases.

Personalised bookshelves,
Home-made decor showcases,

Preserving newspaper clippings,
A vast collection of novels and cook books;
Never overlooked.

The days when cassettes and mix tapes,
Wrapped in wrapping paper and ribbons,
Were predominantly presented to loved ones,
Along with flowers and face to face conversations,
Never in need of social media qualifications.

A time when the 'Real' were preferable,
But oh! the sentimental value of,
A handkerchief given by a loved one;
For me, this can never be outdone.

A real vintage cloth in mint condition,
A handkerchief touched by real love,
My initials inscribed within the art of loving,
Perfectly made rare with an embroidery.

Ripe coloured Sweet-peas and Prim roses,
Swam across the edges, undefiled.
Awaken from time to time,
To breathe in those February hands,
Alongside the stars.

Today I've created a wardrobe of keepsakes,

Contemplating and standing in my home.
Keepsakes of experiences and sentiments,
Of people intertwined and mindful places.
For those of us born in the 1990s,
We live a life filled with sentimental soundtracks,
Playing in the background of our minds.

18. Fired-Up Faith : Even The Rain Moved Away

After an earnest wait upon the Lord,
The unconditional favour came unseen,
Our new journey begins to be,
The merging of past adventures, to form a family.
Like a book with a hard cover,
Our chapters were never left unsheltered;
Even the wilderness and the uncharted waters,
Were overwhelmingly consumed with fierce love.

The happiest moments in life,
When shared with someone we love,
Looks like a perfectly structured flower,
With its undying favourable fragrance.
He said,
He loved the freckle on my face,
And my natural curls called his name.

I felt the Clear night skies spoke of His glory,
A faith filled with the fire of the Holy Spirit,
Alive and on a mission to testify true love.
Despite being a summer night,
The summer sky shone so bright,
The rain moved away.

The wind gave a romantic ambience,
For two hearts to collide.

They say, "Faith is a powerful thing."
So,Yes! we had our Engagement ceremony outside,
A sacred get-together,
The engagement ring on my finger,
The cake cutting splendor,
A prayer to bind two hearts forever,
A night to remember,
In the beginning of May
Which was not really in summer.

The spring goes undercover
And acts more like summer,
I do remember,
Though May is a part of spring,
The whole week has known only summer rain.
With no sun for seven days straight,
It makes my night more summer than spring.
Yet, our faith moved the rain away.

These moments safely Captured,
Witnessed by longing eyes,
Calculated by curious minds.
But instead of the summer rain,
We were soaked in His grace.

The sky our ceiling,
The stars our chandelier,
The smaller stars are light bulbs,
The light bulbs attached to the branches,
The classiest branches of our chandelier.
A summer evening submerged,
Not in rainwater,
But inevitably,
Submerged in God's Favour.

Provided with a friend, a life-partner,
A spiritually armoured warrior.
Consumed in God's Love,
Overwhelmed by His goodness.

Thus, I have to say it again,
Even the wilderness and the uncharted waters,
Were overwhelmingly and victoriously
Consumed with fierce love.

19. Gardenia - The Wedding Poem

For Richard, My Husband

For Richard, my Husband

Your existence appropriately covers me,
Like the fragrance of the Gardenia flower,
Effectively, in the month of October.

From today I'll take the most noble part,
Hand in hand, in this voyage with you.
I'll help carry portions of your triumph,
And portions of your despair,
Not for a moment will I cease to see,
The warm soul-stirring look in your eyes.
The vibrant, fulfilling, thoughtful sound,
Of your voice, amidst the noise.
You will never cease to be,
The man,
Who shattered all my insecurities.

Not for a moment will I cease to comprehend,
Who you are as a man,
Most importantly of who and how,

Our God wanted you to be.

And nowhere but beside you,
I want to honour God for making you mine.
Nowhere but beside you,
I want to listen to the harmonious wind
every summer evening, singing a song,
When that spiritual warfare has been won.

Because with you,
I will always be singing, praying
And praising in the storm.
For I have learnt to merged
with your preferences, your opinions,
your struggles;
I will love you with a heart made pure.

And when seasons of unrevealed conflict comes,
Let me patiently surrender your frailties at His feet,
Let me unveil that delicate side of your personality,
To thoughtfully consider your needs,
Your interests and your integrity.

When we find ourselves unable,
To apprehend the overwhelming knot of difficulty.
Let Him lead us again,
Beside the quiet waters;

My love, I pray, You will be filled with His wisdom,
To live a life worthy of His grace,
To be submerged in the enrichment of your soul.

Your uncompromising love for Christ,
Has awaken the love we have built for each other.
So, I promise to speak only encouragement,
When the pressures of life tries to drown you,
Most of all,
I will nourish my heart to listen,
To appreciate and to truthfully honour you.

If need be,
I am looking at you now,
Clothed in His grace,
Telling you entreatingly,
If we remained in His anointing steadfast love,
Our feet will never grow weary.
And I will stand with you,
As you stand for Him in humility.

With much Love,
 Deima,
Your wife to be.
From October 2023.

20. In Remembrance of the Redolence of Moral Stories

The calm comes from the power of His presence.
Ah! to wonder at the beauty of His Grace;
For I know my maker can hush the darkened noise,
I must bring forth my strongest side,
The scented prowess I mustn't hide,
I will move onward,
Even if the way is dreaded by most.

The deepest yearning in every soul,
Unutterably intensifies,
When soaking in the sunlight with our closed eyes.
Our fragrant character not altered, never impaired,
The astonishing favours of a Christ-filled life.

That longed-for sense of never-ending sunset skies.
The perfumed demeanor of a young child,
Hovering across clueless valleys of untrodden meadows,
Where the unpolluted river never runs dry.

Speaking of a true Christian life,
To express gratitude in times of plunder,
Like the Cedar tree who imparts fragrance even during
its final hours of surrender.

A scent of meaningful origin, its goodness,
So distinctively.
Carried around so silently, under acts of normality.

The most dreaded uncharted lands,
Can be subsided by the presence of the good Shepherd,
So, dear fellow believer,
You can walk out with scented hands,
To help heal a broken brother.

Find a way to rid yourself of that dimly lid depressed
attire,
The dire collection of unsolved forlorn cases.
Like moral stories and life lessons,
Hidden gems in between the pages.
We need to read in between the lines,
The beauty of words hiding in plain sight.

A story was written,
About a Musk Deer and its scented gland,
Hiding a unique content of high demand.
Unaware, he was the source,
He journeyed far to find it.

His efforts drained, it was in vain;
His obsession, "oh, too harsh," he sigh,
A valuable treasure that lies within,

Was left unseen.
Unaware, it was from him, it originated.

He carried around a rare natural thing,
A rich perfume, I presumed,
Stated to be expensive in the human world.
He lived his life,
Each day he lived,
Surrounded by a fragrant-filled air.
He traveled to far off lands,
With eagerness and fearlessness,
To find the source,
The perfect cause,
Of the heavenly aroma fair.

No one could tell him from where it came,
Oh, so affected by the inability there.
Determined to locate the source of joy,
Oh, so enslaved by the burden here.
Definitely stirred to fight the fight,
Against all odds, to make it right.

He failed to think, it could be him,
The source of happy rapture.
Unbearable, he found a cliff,
The edge a welcome favour.

No longer alive, left unrecognised,
His abdomen and entrails didn't matter,
Splattered on the sharp rocks forever.
And for a short while,
The valley was filled,
With the most beautiful fragrance,
Of the natural Musk from within his gland.

The moral of the story here
Holds a different meaning for different minds,
But for me personally, the moral says,
There's so much chaos in this world,
Don't forget, You might get lost,
Led astray by a deep-seated desire.

The darkened noise must be hushed,
Let the calm come nearer.
The calm comes from the power of His presence,
For us to always remember.
The confusing voice, the hesitant choice,
Ceased to follow altogether.
Look closer, within your soul,
There it is, the goal you are after.
The endless chase, the worldly thrill,
They melted away into nothingness,
From the power of our saviour.

21. White Lilies Never Dies Near Aslan's Country

The Silver sea, so beautifully created,
The floating White Lilies seemed to gave out,
A blessed, scented empowerment,
Through the movie screen, as well as,
Through the well-read pages.
A scene so beautiful,
So delightfully scripted,
Led to tearful eyes,
A conviction for clueless hearts,
A repentant lump in our throats.
The longing for heavenly bliss,
Deep-rooted long ago.

Reepicheep, the warrior mouse,
Worked wholeheartedly,
With all sincerity, all his life,
To enter Aslan's Country.
The ultimate goal of his life,
Finally in his grasp.
But he assumed,
He wasn't worthy or faithful enough.
These feelings of doubt, inhumanly rough.

Then, Aslan replied,
*"My country was made for noble hearts such as yours,
no matter how small their bearers be."

Reepicheep courageously reached
Aslan's Country,
His desire, his driving force,
The central goal,
Of every warrior-believer.
In the book,
We can visualise,
A different mouse altogether;
But the movie also portrayed him,
A noble mouse, an honest qualifier.

Near Aslan's Country,
Their voyage came to an end,
A new spiritual journey awakens;
Aspects of the Christian narrative, written.

The useful usage of symbolism,
An allegory and a moral compass,
That encompasses the human heart.
A hidden spiritual message,
Of the operational spiritual realm,
Breaking like the waves on the shore.
Readers, viewers and listeners,

Learned about,
The Christian concept of Christ,
In C.S.Lewis's The Chronicles of Narnia.

Aslan's sacrifice to save Edmund Pevensie,
Represents Christ's love for you and me.
We are a creative generation,
Caught in the web of conventional eyes,
At times, we may be weakened and terrorised,
But we will never be the enslaved caravan,
We will never be the captured clan.

The cracked stone-table echoed,
The image of the empty tomb.
The role of humility in humanity,
The gentle water inside real power.
Aslan,
A figure, so inventively direct,
Designed to paint a picture,
Of the Crucifixion,
And the Resurrection of Jesus Christ.

Aslan spoke to Caspian and the children,
In the book, He told them,
*"But there I have another name.
You must learn to know me by that name."

However, the movie diverted a little,
Establishing Lucy's Faith,
Aslan told Lucy,
Moving His reassuring golden mane,
•"In your World, I have another name,
 You must learn to know me by it."

Aslan, the Lion, in Narnia,
Stands to be, the embodiment,
Of Jesus Christ, our gracious King.
A story of daily happenings,
Of Lucy Pevensie's inability to love herself,
Discovered that her existence
Was on the verge of replacement.
She didn't understand her importance,
She was the one to have found,
The Wardrobe,
The way that led her to her Narnian friends.
Then Aslan spoke wisdom into her,
*"You doubt your value.
Don't run from who you are."

When she heard Him say,
*"Courage, dear heart."
Lucy Pevensie was uplifted,
And set apart.

And who could forget,
Eustace Clarence Scrubb,
Who aimlessly walked,
Unequipped,
On an unexplored island.

*"He falls asleep on a dead dragon's hoard
 and finds himself transformed into a dragon
by "greedy, dragonish thoughts" in his heart."
Eustace couldn't, on his own,
Changed back, even when he wanted to.
He needed the Lion's honourable claw,
To release the curse from his skin.
In due course of time,
Aslan walked towards him,
When Aslan removed the scales,
The hurt begins to enter.
But this pain is a must,
An imperative renovation,
A temporary pain towards permanent gain,
Thereafter.
Like removing a Porcupine quill,
Once they penetrate the attacker,
Their barbed and sharp formation,
Speak potentially of harm,
If left unattended.

But it wasn't difficult for Aslan,
To carefully unfasten, to easily unhand them.
The infected part, required no further infection.
To human form Eustace returned,
When Aslan peeled off his dragon skin.
He later bathe,
Submerged, then significantly emerged,
Refreshed and rejuvenated.
A full body experience,
Like taking a step in water Baptism.

C.S.Lewis himself, wrote,
The characteristics of Aslan,
A parallel figure of the Saviour.
Aslan is the definition of the King,
The King who led his people to salvation,
A conqueror for the downtrodden sojourner.
In The Voyage Of The Dawn Treader,
Aslan finally told them,
* "This was the very reason why
you were brought to Narnia,
That by knowing me here for a little,
You may know me better there."

As the bitter-sweet melancholic
Soundtrack parted,
The movie ended, as expected.

But the consciousness is convinced,
That Narnia was about spiritual awakening,
And never merely about kids exploring nor
About rational animals talking about honour.

Footnotes -
 * - The Asterisk next to the words under the double
inverted commas refers to the original dialogue
extracted from the Books created by C.S.Lewis,
The Chronicles of Narnia.
• - The Bullet point symbol refers to the dialogue in the
movie adaptation of The Chronicles of Narnia.

The quotes in this particular poem are mostly the
original dialogues from the Books,
The dialogue in the movies are mostly the modified
version, often made to suit the cinematic format.
Hence, there is a difference.